3/96

D0932173

A Salute to Black Pioneers

ISBN 0-922162-3-4 (Volume III)
ISBN 0-922162-15-8 (Volume Set)

A Salute to Black Pioneers

EMPAK PUBLISHING COMPANY

Publisher & Editor: Richard L. Green
Assoc. Editor: Dorothy M. Love-Carroll
Researcher: Ted Evans
Production: Dickinson & Associates, Inc.
Illustration: S. Gaston Dodson
Foreword: Dr. Charles A. Taylor

Lift Every Voice And Sing

Lift every voice and sing
Till the earth and heaven ring.
Ring with the harmonies of Liberty;
Let our rejoicing rise
High as the listening skies,
Let it resound loud as the rolling sea.
Sing a song full of the faith that the
    dark past has taught us,
Sing a song full of the faith that the
    present has brought us,
Facing the rising sun of our new day begun,
Let us march on till victory is won.

James Weldon Johnson

On behalf of Empak Publishing Company, I am pleased to endorse the third in a special series of Black History publications: *A Salute to Black Pioneers*, produced by Empak. This booklet gives positive recognition to Black Americans who played significant roles in the shaping of early American civilization.

It is appropriate that Empak has chosen to bring forth *A Salute to Black Pioneers* as its third booklet. Benjamin Quarles, the noted scholar in the field of American Negro history, once stated; "Things that one knows about the past, are of consequence in shaping his present and in giving contours to the future." On this note, the denying of Black history, over the years, has played a major role in the oppression and suppression of today's Black America. Our Black ancestors, through their pioneering spirit, hardships, perseverance, vision, ingenuity and application, were indeed instrumental in the building of this great land--a factor that, once made known and fully understood by our youth, will serve as a major guiding influence.

Benjamin Quarles further stated; "When our history books do not mention the Negro, significant omissions result. When he is mentioned solely with reference to problem areas, an incomplete, distorted picture emerges. In either case a more balance focus is desirable." The biographical grouping of the Black pioneers, contained within this booklet, provides a balanced of the scope and magnitude of Blacks' indisputable accomplishments and contributions to early America. Overcoming obstacles of poverty, prejudice and often poor education, immense land was owned; trails were blazed; treaties were signed; territories were conquered; personal rights were acquired; and considerable wealth was amassed by many of our forefathers. The Black presence in America has been felt in virtually every field of human endeavor.

The *A Salute to Black Pioneers* is an educational jewel that will touch Black America's heart with worthy pride. I commend Empak Publishing Company for affording you and me the opportunity to acquaint ourselves with these historic Black pioneers. This booklet further serves as a testimony that all things are possible, providing there is vision, hard work, and faith in God.

Dr. Charles A. Taylor

EDITOR'S NOTE: In his own right, Dr Charles A. Taylor, educator and author, has also made significant contributions to Black America. He is the Assistant Dean of Students, Black Student Advisor and Lecturer in Afro-American Studies at Loyola University of Chicago; member of the National Association of Student Personnel Administrators; and listed in*Outstanding Young Men In America* and *Who's Who in the Midwest.*

CONTENTS

BIOGRAPHIES:

Editor's Note: Due to this booklet's space limitations, some facets on the lives of the above noted Historic Black Pioneers have been omitted.

DR. CARTER G. WOODSON
1875-1950

Dr. Carter G. Woodson, a Harvard Ph.D., was an editor, educator, author and the "father of modern Negro historiography." He was also the founder of the Association for the Study of Negro Life and History, the Associated Publishers, and the Journal Of Negro History. In 1926, he initiated Negro History Week, which later evolved into Black History Month in 1976.

Woodson was born in New Canton, Virginia, December 19, 1875, to newly freed slaves, James and Anne Eliza Woodson, and was the oldest of nine children. His family was extremely poor, and had to rely on Woodson's small wages from his work in the coal mines. When he was 17, his family relocated to Fayette, Virginia. He took another job in the coal mines, but was permitted to attend Douglass High part-time. He completed his course work in a year-and-a-half, graduating in 1896.

Thereafter, Woodson entered Berea College, in Kentucky, and soon returned to Douglass High as its principal, serving from 1900 to 1903. In the meantime, he took correspondence courses, attended summer/autumn sessions at the University of Chicago, receiving a B.A. degree in 1907, and an M.A. degree in 1908.

During the period of 1903 to 1909, he served as supervisor of schools in the Philippines. He traveled to Asia, North Africa, and Europe, completing extensive course work and becoming proficient in Spanish and French. Back in the States, while in residence at Harvard University, he taught English, Spanish, French and history at Dunbar High in Washington, D.C., from 1909 to 1918. While teaching, he also did research at the Library of Congress for his doctoral dissertation, *The Disruption of Virginia*, and received his Ph.D. from Harvard in 1912.

As a result of his years of study and research, Dr. Woodson came to realize that the Black man's past contributions had to be documented and taught. He concluded that if a race had no recorded history, its achievements would be forgotten and, in time, claimed by other groups. He found that many of the achievements by Blacks were overlooked, ignored and even suppressed by writers of history textbooks.

It was Woodson's dream that the truth would be revealed as to Afro-Americans' contributions to the discovery, pioneering, development, and continuance of America. His prime ambition was that young Blacks would grow up with a firm knowledge of their ancestors. One of his most popular text books, *The Negro In Our History*, was widely used for years in high schools, colleges, and universities.

Dr. Woodson was often ridiculed for his efforts. At one time, large foundations were encouraged to withdraw funding of over $100,000 in support of the ASNLH, which evolved into the Association for the Study of Afro-American Life and History (ASALH). Taking full burden of his cause, with perseverance and vision, Dr. Woodson researched, sorted and compiled voluminous information about the American Negro. The ASNLH held its first meeting in Chicago in 1915. The following year, from this association sprung the publication of the *Journal Of Negro History*, a scientific quarterly. Dr. Woodson served as director and editor of this publication until his death.

From 1919 to 1920, Dr. Woodson served as dean of the School of Liberal Arts and head of the graduate faculty at Howard University. For the next two years, he was dean of West Virginia Collegiate Institute. In 1922, he retired from college teaching and spent the rest of his life writing, editing and promoting Black history.

On April 3, 1950, Dr. Carter G. Woodson died. Although he produced no offspring, he fathered the recording of a people's history and nurtured its growth and development into recognition and acceptance.

ABRAHAM
c.1790 to after 1870

Abraham was a fugitive slave, adopted by the Seminole Indians in 1826. Although uneducated, he was a persuasive and gifted speaker. He was spokesman for Chief Micanopy during the period when the United States was relocating the Indians from Florida to Oklahoma and Kansas. He was referred to by the Indians as the "prophet, high chancellor, and keeper of the King's conscience."

Abraham was born to slavery in Pensacola, Florida, about 1790. He was reported to be a full-blooded Negro of large and powerful stature with a "cast" in his right eye. Although no parental information is recorded, records do indicate that Abraham married and fathered a daughter and two sons. In the early 1820s, he ran away and took shelter with the Seminole Indians. The Seminoles were a collection of many different tribes, who banded together in the Florida swamps, and they provided a sanctuary to hundreds of run-away slaves.

Abraham played a key role in both the Seminole Indian War and in their peace negotiations with the U.S. Government. It was said that he ruled all the councils of the Indians through his influence over the chief. However, his main concern was for the Blacks who lived among the Seminoles; therefore, he opposed and blocked the relocating of the Indians for years. He feared that, while traveling across southern territory, many fugitives would be recaptured by their former masters. During the peace negotiations, he wanted a guarantee that his people would not be returned to slavery once they left the Indian sanctuary.

In 1826, as prime minister and privy counselor to Chief Micanopy, Abraham accompanied the Chief to Washington, D.C. to negotiate relocation plans. In 1832, as interpreter for the Seminoles, he witnessed the signing of the removal treaty. In 1833, Abraham went with the Seminole delegation to investigate the proposed site of the Indians' new home. For the next two years, he served as interpreter at all councils at which United States agents insisted on the Seminole's removal. Not trusting the U.S. delegation, Abraham secretly encouraged Chief Micanopy to resist. Meanwhile, Abraham stashed a supply of guns and ammunition and enlisted the support of the plantation slaves of the region.

Relocation plans collapsed when the Indians learned they had been tricked, and hostilities broke out December 28, 1835. Abraham proved to be a cunning and brave warrior, both feared and respected by the U.S. Army. During two years of bloody war, he and his Black and Indian warriors fought General T. S. Jesup's soldiers all through the Florida swamps, and at one time wiped out an entire company of Jesup's men.

Abraham, expecting to be hanged, had "decided to die if he must, like a man, in one more effort to save his people." Fortunately, Abraham was as wise as he was brave. Seeing that relocation was inevitable, he and two Seminole Chiefs, Jumper and Alligator, agreed to a peace conference with Jesup in 1837. Due to Abraham's diplomatic finesse, an agreement was made for the Seminoles to relocate, accompanied by their Black allies.

Later, the assumed treaty was broken by White agents and hostilities resumed. Under the threat of hanging by government agents, Abraham continued to work for peace. Working through Chief Micanopy, he brought about the surrender and compliance of the other Chiefs; and later in 1837, a second treaty was signed, with a protection clause for Blacks.

By 1839, the Seminoles and Abraham moved west, and Abraham slowly sank into obscurity. In 1870, it was reported that he was a prosperous cattle rancher who lived on the Little River. U.S. officers, who reported on the Seminole War, all agreed on Abraham's intelligence, and described him as "obviously a great man."

Crispus Attucks, a seaman and patriot, was the first American to die in the struggle for American independence during the historic Boston Massacre in 1770.

Crispus Attucks was born to slavery about 1723, in Framingham, Massachusetts. Very little is known about his early life. His father was of African descent and his mother was an Indian. At the age of 27, he ran away, became a seaman on a whaling ship and taught himself to read and write. He applied his acquired knowledge to understanding the underlying principles of government. Having been a slave, he was willing to avenge oppression to extreme measures even to death.

Dissension between the American colonies and the British Empire began around 1761. Later, in 1765, the *Stamp Act* was passed, which made the colonies pay for the British Army stationed in America. Congress was outraged. A statement was issued: "It is inseparably essential to the freedom of a people ... that no taxes be imposed upon them, but with their own consent. . . ." In 1767, the *Townshend Act* placed taxes on tea and other goods and proved to be a serious blow to the dignity of America. Congress said, "Let Great Britain rescind her measures, or the colonies are lost to her forever."

Merchants from all the colonies pledged to boycott all British goods until the act was rescinded. To further enforce the *Townshend Act*, in 1768, two regiments of "redcoats" arrived. In a series of letters, Samuel Adams stated, "To quarter troops on the people, without consent of the Assembly, was a gross violation of the *Bill of Rights*." The people grew tired of second class treatment, oppression, tyranny, and "taxation without representation." This was the state of affairs at the beginning of 1770, before the making of an undying account in American history.

Attucks was a muscular giant who stood several inches over six-feet. He also possessed remarkable qualities of leadership. He was aware of how the Bostonians felt, and knew well the arrogance of the British soldiers. Once when a slight incidence of words occurred between a few young men and a sentry, a crowd, led by Attucks, collected and tempers flared. Oppressed and oppressor came face-to-face. Attucks, however obscure his origin, played a prominent role in the American Revolution. As a symbol of resistance to tyranny, his leadership placed him among the immortals.

On the evening of March 5, 1770, the bells of the city tolled a sad foreshadowing of bloodshed and war. At the same time, freedom and independence beckoned around the corner. The townspeople ran, crying out in agony from past injustices. British soldiers stood with bayonets fixed. Attucks and his followers appeared with clubs and Attucks shouted, "The way to get rid of these soldiers is to attack the main guard! Strike at their roots!"

The first shot, fired by a British soldier, killed Crispus Attucks instantly. The second shot killed a comrade stepping forward to assist Attucks. In all, five people were killed. Seven British soldiers, along with their chief commander, were tried for murder. Daniel Webster said in later years, "From that moment, we may date the severance of the British empire. The patriotic fire kindled in the breasts of those earnest and true men, never was quenched after the massacre until the invaders had been driven from the land and independence had been achieved."

It was not until November 14, 1888, that the officials of the time had assured themselves that they had gathered enough research to erect a monument to this Black man, who had sacrificed his life for America, and "brought about the preliminary victory of the American Revolution." The death of Crispus Attucks, on March 5, 1770, is synonymous with the birth of an independent nation, America.

JAMES PIERSON BECKWOURTH
1798-1866

James P. Beckwourth was a mountain man of the Rocky Mountain regions. He was a colorful, legendary character who loved high adventure. Beckwourth explored the wide expanses of the west, years before the famed "Pathfinder," General John C. Fremont crossed the Rocky Mountains.

One-time chief of the Crow Nation, Beckwourth was an expert fur trapper, trader, scout, Indian fighter, and discoverer of an important mountain pass through the Sierra Nevada Mountains, which bears his name, "Beckwourth Pass."

Beckwourth was born in Fredericksburg, Virginia, on April 6, 1798, the third of thirteen children. His father was a White officer in the Revolutionary War, and his mother was a Negro slave in the service of his father's household. He completed four years of schooling, and later was apprenticed to a "hard-bitten" blacksmith in St. Louis for five years. At 18, he ran away, and had trouble finding work because of his mixed blood. In 1823, he joined the expedition of General William Henry Ashley's Rocky Mountain Fur Trading Company, which penetrated the western wilderness.

The exploits of mountain men are legendary and James P. Beckwourth was among the greatest. Although his life story is full of tales and exciting adventure, as were those of his White peers, Beckwourth's biographer forgot to mention that Beckwourth was a Black man. Unlike his White contemporaries: Kit Carson, Jim Bridger, Davy Crockett and Daniel Boone, all of whom rose to prominence, the invincible Jim Beckwourth was all but deleted from the pages of history. Beckwourth's biographer stated, "Probably no man ever lived who had met with more personal adventure involving danger to life."

Beckwourth became an excellent hunter and expert fur trader. He quickly picked up the ways of the Indians and learned to speak their language. He became a crack shot who never wasted a bullet, and he also handled a bowie knife and tomahawk with ease. He was accepted by the Blackfoot and the Crow Indian tribes and became one of the greatest Indian fighters of his times.

Beckwourth left Ashley's expedition in 1825, and went to live among the Indians for six years. He was adopted by the Crow Nation, when an old squaw insisted he was her long-lost son. "Even if I should deny my Crow origin," said Beckwourth, "They would not believe me." The Crows made him a chieftain and called him "Bull's Robe." He became a mighty warrior and took part in their intertribal wars and, according to Beckwourth, "lifted the scalp of many an enemy."

In 1837, Beckwourth grew tired of the native life, returned to civilization, and established two trading posts. He fought in the Seminole War in 1842, and the California Revolution in 1846. In 1848, traveling with his wife, he met General John C. Fremont and became his chief scout. On this expedition (1850), Beckwourth made a discovery that "should forever secure him a place in Western history."

Just a few miles northwest of what is now Reno, Nevada, Beckwourth found an important pass through the Sierra Nevadas. He personally led the first wagon train of settlers through "Beckwourth Pass," followed later by thousands of pioneers and gold seekers to the fields of California. The Western Pacific Railway later used the "Beckwourth Pass" as a gateway to the west.

Beckwourth's last adventure took place, in 1866, when he fought in the Cheyenne War. He died in Denver, the same year, of mysterious causes. Legend has it that the Crows honored him at a farewell feast to propose that he stay with them and lead them to greatness again. He refused, and it is said that the Crows poisoned him to keep his body and powerful spirit within their land.

CLARA BROWN
c.1803-1885

Clara Brown was a leading pioneer of Colorado. She was a nurse, managed a successful laundry business, and is credited with starting the first Sunday School in her area. She is further credited with the courage of trying to bring law and order to a frontier mining community where prostitution, shoot-outs and murders were common.

Clara was born a slave in Gallatin, Tennessee, in 1803, but grew up in Kentucky. Later, she married and bore four children. One child died at birth; and the rest of the family was separated at a slave auction and were taken by different masters to various parts of the country in 1835. For over twenty years, with the help of her new master, she tried unsuccessfully to find members of her family. In 1857, she contributed $100.00 toward her own freedom when her master died, and at the age of 55, resumed her search once again.

The attraction of the Colorado gold rush, in 1859, was tremendous. The "Fifty-Niners," as they were called, had arrived a hundred thousand strong. Every kind of person imaginable flooded the region: prospectors, settlers, outlaws, gamblers, confidence men, and prostitutes. Most had come in search of their fortune, but Clara Brown had come for a different reason, in search of her family.

After hearing a report that one daughter, Eliza, may have moved west,"Aunt Clara" (as she was known) took a job as a cook on a wagon train headed to Colorado. She was the only Black of six women on the 600-mile trek, which took eight weeks. Aunt Clara walked most of the way. She settled in Denver for a short while, and later went to Central City to find work among the miners. She started a laundry business with boilers and hot tubs that she had brought with her.

Aunt Clara turned her home into a refuge for the impoverished who poured into the camp. It served as a hospital for the physically ill, a church for those who needed spiritual solace, and a hotel for those with no place to stay. Some gave her a small contribution, but those who could not afford to pay were not turned away. Under her direction, the camp's first Sunday School was founded.

In making the long trip to Colorado, she had two important resolves in mind: to become financially independent, and to use her wealth to find her family. By the end of the Civil War, she had managed to save the tidy sum of $10,000. She made some wise investments in Colorado real estate, and left for Virginia and Kentucky in search of her loved ones.

When she returned to Central City, she had found 34 members of her family; she also financed the return fares of 16 other freed slaves. Some of the slaves were orphans. Later, she found jobs for them. Unfortunately, she had not found her daughter. In 1882, the unexpected occurred, Aunt Clara received a report that Eliza was well and living in Council Bluffs, Iowa. The quest ended; mother and daughter met in a tearful but happy reunion which was widely publicized in midwestern newspapers.

In 1885, the hard-working, thrifty and compassionate "Aunt Clara Brown" died in Denver, at the age of 82. She left a warm feeling in the hearts of all who knew her. The Colorado Pioneers Association buried her with honors, and her friends made sure her unlimited charitable deeds would not be forgotten. A plaque was placed in the St. James Methodist Church, telling the story of how her home was the birthplace of the first church in the area. Further, believing her to be the first Black in the city, a seat in the city's Opera House was named for her.

The Colorado Pioneers Association stated in her eulogy that Clara Brown was "the kind of old friend whose heart always responded to the cry of distress and who, rising from the humble position of slave to the angelic type of noble woman, won our sympathy and commanded our respect."

GEORGE WASHINGTON BUSH
c.1790-1863

George W. Bush was an entrepreneur, and an early American explorer of the Oregon territory. He roamed the uncharted west as a fur trader, and is also noted for organizing and leading the first colony of Americans to settle on the shores of Puget Sound.

George was born free in Pennsylvania about 1790. Little is known about his life before 1812, when he fought in the Battle of New Orleans under the command of Andrew Jackson. After his military stint, he worked for a French fur trader headquartered in St. Louis, and later for the Hudson Bay Company, which took him on extended travels to the Pacific coast in the 1820s.

Upon his return, Bush bought a farm in 1831, married Isabella James, who was of German-American descent, and raised a family of five sons. During the spring of 1844, Bush and his family, along with a small group of White settlers headed west. Bush, who carried more than $2,000 in silver, was the wealthiest man among them.

Bush's previous knowledge of the West made him the most valuable member of the group. Several neighbors were able to join the wagon train because Bush, personally, purchased wagons, mule teams and supplies for them. The westward journey was long and rugged. Bush advised the men, "Boys, you are going through a hard country. You have guns and ammunition. Anything you see as big as a blackbird, kill it and eat it." His humanity, shrewd intelligence, and knowledge of the surrounding natives and elements had a great deal to do with carrying the first American settlers through the many crises of famine and war along the way. They reached Oregon territory in late fall, 1844.

Ironically, the racial discrimination Bush thought he had escaped in Missouri was alive and functioning in Oregon. Oregon was admitted to the Union with a Black exclusion law, which forbade Blacks to settle in the area. However, Bush had made friends among the French Canadians and Indians on his previous trips west. Because of this friendship, he and his companions were allowed to cross the Columbia River into Canadian territory and settle where other American emigrants had been denied.

Once settled at Puget Sound, Bush used his money to buy tools and supplies for the settlers. He staked his claim on a 640-acre plot and started a farm which came to be known as "Bush Prairie." His crops flourished and he became the main supplier of fruits, vegetables and grains to the newcomers of the area. During the winter of 1852, the grain supply was low and prices sky-rocketed. Many farmers sold their crops to speculators without regard for their less fortunate neighbors. Bush refused, saying, "I will keep my grain so my neighbor will have enough to live on. I do not intend to see them want for anything I can provide them with." He saved many lives during that winter of famine.

Again, irony played a cruel trick. As the first American settler on Puget Sound, Bush's presence served as the basis of the United States' claim to the land of the "49th Parallel," a boundary dispute between the U.S. and Britain. Bush's property was once again within Oregon territory. All he had worked for was in jeopardy. His White friends, whom he had refused to exploit, took a stand on his behalf. Collectively, they used their influence to petition Congress to grant Bush a title to his land, and their efforts proved fruitful in 1855, only eight years before his death.

George W. Bush died in 1863. His sons inherited his property, and carried on the family tradition of excellent farming skills and public service. They maintained the same high respect and goodwill of the settlement. One son raised a prize wheat crop which was exhibited at the Smithsonian Institute in Washington, D.C. A second son, William Owen, served two terms in the Washington State House of Representatives.

PAUL CUFFEE
1759-1817

Paul Cuffee, a true pioneer, was a wealthy merchant-mariner, ship-builder and humanitarian. He is best known for his efforts in colonizing Sierra Leone, in Africa, with free Blacks from the United States.

Cuffee was born on the island of Cutty Hunk, near New Bedford, Massachusetts, in 1759, the seventh of 10 children and the youngest of 4 sons. His father, Cuffee Slocum, was a former slave and his mother, Ruth Moses, was an Indian. Paul's father died when Paul was 13, Paul later changed his last name to Cuffee, his father's first name. When Paul's father died, he left an unproductive farm to Paul and a brother; they later sold the farm to try other pursuits.

Cuffee's interest in the sea motivated him to learn to read and write in order to pursue navigational studies. In 1783, he married Alice Pequit, of his mother's Indian tribe, and they later had two daughters and six sons. Going to sea at 16 enabled Cuffee to purchase a farm, for $3,500, on the east branch of the Westport river. His second voyage was to the West Indies.

During his third voyage, which was after the start of the American Revolution, Cuffee was captured by the British and kept prisoner in New York City for three months. After his release, he returned to his farm and decided to build his own vessels and become a trader. Cuffee made five unsuccessful attempts at securing his trading business, but each time pirates set upon him, seizing his boats and cargo.

After the Revolution, the trading business became stable and he was able to establish a profitable trade. With his profits from smaller ventures, and a partner, Cuffee built larger and better ships, which he used for whaling and the coastal shipping of fish, corn and other cargo. In 1793, he built the *Mary*, a 42-ton schooner; in 1795, the 69-ton *Ranger* was completed; in 1808, the *Hero* was added; and in 1810, the 268-ton *Alpha* and 109-ton brig, the *Traveller*, were added to his fleet. In addition to these vessels, Cuffee owned considerable real estate.

Cuffee's wealth in no way diminished his concern for the Black cause. He built a school on his farm, hired a teacher, and opened it to the public. He and his brother petitioned the Massachusetts legislative body, and an *Act* was passed granting to the free Blacks all the privileges of White citizens, including the right to vote. Thus, Paul Cuffee's efforts permanently influenced the welfare of the entire Black population of North America.

It was the popular belief, at the time, that African colonization was the answer to the plight of free Blacks in America. Paul Cuffee was a firm supporter of this assertion. In early 1810, Captain Cuffee, as he was known by then, was given a letter of endorsement from the Society of Friends, for him to sail to Sierra Leone to make observations concerning the desirability of free Blacks settling there. War between America and the English delayed his plans for another trip to Sierra Leone.

However, on December 5, 1815, with 38 Black Americans and considerable cargo aboard the *Traveller*, Cuffee was able to return. He personally paid the passage ($4,000) for 30 of the passengers. Captain Cuffee returned to America on June 1, 1816. Unfortunately, before he could make additional plans, his health failed. Captain Paul Cuffee died September 9, 1817.

■■■ JEAN BAPTISTE POINTE DuSABLE ■■■
c.1745-1818

DuSable was a famous frontier trader, fur trapper, farmer, businessman and the "authenticated father" of the nation's third largest city, Chicago.

Historical records do not agree as to the origin of this great man. However, tradition insists that DuSable was born a free Black, about 1745, in St. Marc, Saint Dominque (Haiti). He was the son of a French mariner and an African-born slave mother. His father took him to France to be educated, and afterwards, he worked as a seaman on his father's ships. He was a handsome man, powerfully built (over six feet), well-educated and cultured. He had a love for European art and at one time owned 23 old world art treasures. He spoke French, English, Spanish, and several Indian dialects.

At the age of 20, DuSable was injured on a voyage to New Orleans. Upon reaching the shores of New Orleans (then French territory), he learned that the Spanish government had taken over. The French Jesuits, a Catholic order, protected DuSable from being enslaved until he was well enough to make his way up the Mississippi River. He later settled in Peoria, Illinois.

In the early 1770s, DuSable built a cabin and eventually owned more than 800 acres of land in Peoria. He enjoyed a special relationship with the Illinois territorial Indians. He took a Potawatomi Indian, Catherine, as his common-law wife and fathered a daughter, Susanne, and a son, Jean. Some years later, he left Peoria and made his way north until he reached the Great Lakes area.

The promise of greatness of the "Chicago" area, on which DuSable decided to settle, had been passed over by others before him. None had the foresight to look beyond its barren, damp, marshy condition, nor did they have the fortitude to make "nothing" into one of the greatest locations in the western hemisphere.

In 1779, starting from scratch, DuSable built the first permanent home on the north bank of the Chicago River, where the present-day Tribune Tower stands. It was a well-constructed house consisting of five rooms and equipped with all the modern conveniences of the times. Later, despite the disadvantages, DuSable established a thriving trading post and, in short time, became well-known as far away as Wisconsin and Detroit. The trading post consisted of a mill, bakehouse, dairy, smokehouse, workshop, poultry house, horse stable, barn and several other smaller buildings. His post was the main supply station for White trappers, traders, woodsmen, and the Indians.

The Chicago portage boomed. It became the key route for merchant trading, and DuSable sent wheat, breads, meats and furs to trading posts in Detroit and Canada. DuSable became a man of considerable wealth and means. He also owned a substantial quantity of field and carpentry tools, which indicated that he must have hired men for field work and building assignments. In addition, he owned an appreciable quantity of livestock, poultry and hogs.

In 1784, DuSable brought his wife and children to Chicago. And, as DuSable was a devout Catholic, he and Catherine were properly married by a Catholic priest. In 1796, their grand-daughter became the first child born in the city of Chicago. As the history of DuSable unfolds, it leaves all history scholars puzzled by his sudden departure from such a prosperous environment. On May 7, 1800, the "father" of Chicago sold his entire wealth for a mere $1,200 and left the area. In 1818, he died almost penniless, and was buried in a Catholic cemetery in St. Charles, Missouri.

Today, on this land, "which DuSable once owned by right of toil," stands the Wrigley Building, Sun-Times Building, Equitable Building, Chicago's main Public Library, and the beginning of the "Magnificent Mile." Within Chicago, a city plaque, a public high school and a museum bear the honorable DuSable name.

ESTEBAN
?-1539

Esteban, sometimes called Estevanico, was born in Azamor, a city in Morocco, Africa. He was a famed pioneer and explorer. Only 45 years after Columbus discovered America, he became the first Black man to lead a Spanish expedition to explore the American southwest. In this momentous overland journey, Esteban discovered what are now the states of Arizona and New Mexico.

It is believed that Esteban was between 28 and 30 years-old when he joined the Narveaz expedition, which sailed from San Lucas de Barrameda, Spain, June 17, 1527.

Esteban was part of a company of 600 men to land on the coast of Florida. For three months they were harassed and many were killed by hostile Indians. In September 1527, the remaining 240 men of the expedition set sail in a number of small boats from the Gulf of Mexico. By the end of the year, there were only four survivors left, three Whites and the Negro Esteban. They wandered among the native Indians for eight years. During this time, they suffered incredible misery and privation. They were enslaved and endured vile, barbaric abuse. But Esteban learned the Indian dialect and picked up their characteristics. He became a medicine man and healer, and was later held in high esteem. The Indians came from great distances to be cured and crowds began following Esteban wherever he went.

When the four survivors were found by Spanish soldiers in 1536, they had made a remarkable journey from Florida, across the continent to the Gulf of California, almost to the Pacific Ocean. And in that journey, they had become the first explorers to discover the vast empty land of Texas and northern Mexico. They were taken to Mexico City where they reported stories to the Viceroy of Spain, Antonia de Mendoza, about a wealthy city encrusted in jewels, called the "Seven Cities of Cibola." Mendoza believed in the tale of the Seven Cities with heart and soul.

Mendoza selected a Franciscan friar, Fray Marcos de Niza, and a guide, Esteban, to make the historic journey on March 7, 1539. They were accompanied by several hundred friendly Indians. Esteban and his party set out and, after some weeks, reached a savage land where Black nor White had ever been before. Esteban became impatient with the slow progression of the godly friar and decided to press ahead. Depending on the size and importance of his discoveries, Esteban agreed that he would send back word in the sign of varying crosses because he was illiterate.

After about four days, one of Esteban's Indian aides staggered into the friar's camp bearing a cross as tall as a man, bellowing, "I have made a great discovery." Come immediately was the meaning. Dressed in barbaric Indian splendor, wearing colorful mantles decorated with gay feathers, jingling bells, and closely followed by two fierce greyhounds, Esteban crossed the vast deserts of Arizona where no man had ever set foot. Soon thereafter, he saw the gates of the Seven Cities of the Zuni Indians. Esteban had discovered New Mexico.

Esteban sent a peace offering by a messenger, seeking counsel with the Zuni chief. In response, the Chief replied, "Tell your lord, you will all be killed." At sunrise the following morning, Esteban approached the gate and was immediately "transfixed with Cibola arrows" (1539). Only two of his Indian scouts made their escape and fearfully returned to the friar, reporting Estaban's ill fate.

One historian states, "The value of the discovery was such that we can only rightfully accord to Esteban an important place among the early explorers of America." Further importance can be added in that previous expeditions had been planned for the uncharted southwest, but had failed.

MARY FIELDS
1832-1914

In all the west, Mary Fields had no equal. She was a 6-foot, 200-pound, cigar-smoking, guntotin' pioneer who settled her arguments with her fists, and once in a while with her sixshooter. The folks around Cascade, Montana, knew her as a freight hauler, laundress, restaurant owner, and the second female ever to drive a United States mail coach.

Mary Fields was born a slave on May 15, 1832. A free spirit, she decided that slavery was not for her and ran away to Toledo, Ohio. She found work in a convent and formed a close attachment to Mother Amadeus. When the sisters headed to Montana, to undertake the monumental task of christianizing Indian tribes, Mary remained in Toledo. En route, Mother Amadeus fell seriously ill with pneumonia and Mary undertook the hazardous journey to her friend's bedside.

After Mother Amadeus recovered, Mary remained in Montana to help the sisters build a school, which took eight severe winters. Mary did all the hard work. She also served as protector for the nuns. She was never without her .38 Smith & Wesson strapped under her apron, and her shotgun was ever-ready. They said, "Black Mary," as she was sometimes called, "couldn't miss a thing within 50 paces." And, they also said she could whip any two men in the territory.

Because of the extreme cold, Mary dressed like a man, except for a long dress and apron she wore over a pair of men's pants. This covering for her 200 pound-plus frame made her an unforgettable sight to behold. On at least two memorable occasions, Mary engaged in warfare with men of the area. Once, a neighborhood derelict made a face and other certain insulting gestures at her. Mary adorned his face with a stone, and he was last seen sprinting toward the general direction of the Canadian border.

On another occasion, Mary was involved in a shoot-out with a hired hand, as was the tradition of the Old West. Mary placed her bullet too close for his comfort, and the man took the hint and fled. Mary held her own in the presence of men and beasts. One night, she was returning to the mission with supplies when her horses were frightened by wolves. She was found the next morning sitting on the upturned wagon, shot gun poised, guarding her team and supplies.

The nuns loved Mary in spite of her behavior. And although she had served the mission for 10 years without receiving a penny of compensation, the Bishop decided her wild ways were too much and sent her away in 1895. Mary and the nuns were heartbroken. Mother Amadeus helped Mary open a restaurant in Cascade twice, and both attempts failed because Mary was too free-hearted with her non-paying customers. Afterwards, Mother Amadeus asked the government to give Mary a mail route. Mary made her triumphant deliveries to the mission seated on top of the mail coach smoking a huge cigar. She held this job for eight years, never missing a day, and later became known as "Stage Coach Mary."

Mary retired and opened a laundry business in her home. One day while idling in the local saloon, she saw a man who owed her money for a laundry bill. After knocking the man down, she announced: "His laundry bill is paid." At that time, she was well into her seventies. The townspeople loved Mary. The mayor gave her special permission to drink in saloons with men, and the owner of the Cascade Hotel gave strict orders that Mary Fields was to receive her meals free. Because she couldn't remember her exact birthday, she celebrated twice a year.

Whenever Mary decided to have a birthday, town officials would close the school in her honor. When fire destroyed her home in 1912, so esteemed was she that the townspeople re built it at their expense. Mary Fields died in 1914, and was mourned by the entire population of Cascade, Montana. The exploits of Mary Fields are legendary; and "legends never die."

BARNEY FORD
c.1824-1902

Barney Ford, an early pioneer in Colorado, was a businessman, wealthy hotel owner and restaurateur, political activist, and conductor of the Underground Railroad in Chicago, Illinois.

Ford was born a slave in Virginia, in 1824. When he was 18, his owner hired him out as a waiter on a Mississippi steamboat. He escaped, and with the help of the Underground Railroad, he went to Chicago where he met Henry Wagoner. Both men taught themselves to read and write, and Ford later married Wagoner's sister, Julia, and fathered three children. He worked with the Underground Railroad until he heard that gold had been discovered in California, in 1848.

Since Ford was a fugitive slave, he was fearful of traveling overland. He bought ship passage to California for himself and Julia, by way of Nicaragua. Central America proved to be an ideal place for making money, and Ford decided to stay. In 1851, he opened the United States Hotel and Restaurant, playing host to many United States dignitaries. During a political dispute with Great Britain, an American ship bombarded the town, destroying his hotel and half of the city. Ford and his wife returned to Chicago $5,000 richer. He opened a livery stable which doubled as a station for the Underground Railroad.

In 1860, Ford headed west again to Colorado, in search of gold. En route, he was denied a seat on a stagecoach and had to go by wagon train. He was refused a hotel room in Mountain City, and boarded with the famous Aunt Clara Brown. He staked a claim near Denver, but it was jumped by White men. He and several other Black prospectors staked another claim on a hill southeast of Breckinridge, Colorado.

Since the *Dred Scott* court decision denied Blacks the right to own land, Ford asked his White lawyer to file a claim in the lawyer's name. Assuming Ford had struck it rich, the lawyer sent the sheriff to order Ford off "his land" within twenty-four hours. That night, White riders came and ran Ford and his friends away. The White men were unable to find gold, and afterwards started the legend that Ford had buried it on the mountainside, which they named "Nigger Hill." In 1964, it was historically named, "Barney Ford Hill."

Ford returned to Denver and soon became a prosperous tycoon in the hotel, restaurant and barber shop businesses. His luxurious Inter-Ocean Hotels, in Denver and Cheyenne, were the fanciest hotels in the West, and his impressive guest list included President Ulysses S. Grant. By the 1870s, Ford had amassed a fortune estimated at close to a quarter of a million dollars. Ford's influence was felt in many ways. During the Civil War, he gave financial assistance, food, and jobs to run-away and newly freed slaves. With his friend Wagoner, he established Colorado's first adult education classes for Blacks. They taught Blacks reading, writing, arithmetic, and the principles of democratic government.

In support of the Black cause, Ford joined the fight and lobbied in Washington over the organization of the Colorado territory and the question of statehood. Ford's battle against statehood was to prevent Blacks' loss of citizenship in Colorado. Primarily due to his lobbying efforts, Colorado lost its initial bid for statehood. Later, he became the first Black to serve on a Colorado grand jury. And, in 1882, he and his wife were the first Blacks to be invited to a Colorado Association of Pioneers' dinner. Ford, who championed the Black cause all of his life, died of a stroke in 1902.

Her given name was Nancy Green, but the world knew her as"Aunt Jemima." Although the famous Aunt Jemima recipe was not hers, she became the advertising world's first living trademark. She was born a slave in Montgomery County, Kentucky in 1834.

In 1889, the Aunt Jemima Pancake Mix was introduced in St,. Joseph, Missouri after Chris L. Rutt, a newspaperman, and Charles G. Underwood bought the Pearl Milling Company. Searching for a novel product to survive in a highly competitive business, the two men hit on the original idea of developing and packaging a ready-mixed, self-rising pancake flour.

In the fall of 1889, Rutt attended a vaudeville show where he heard a catchy tune called, "Aunt Jemima," sung by a blackfaced performer, clad in apron and bandanna headband. Soon after, the whole town was humming the song, and Rutt immediately decided that Aunt Jemima was the name for his pancake mix. Short on capital, Rutt and Underwood went broke and sold the formula to the R.T. Davis Milling Company in 1890. Davis decided to try a new idea, and began looking for a Negro woman to employ as a living trademark for his new product. He found Nancy Green in Chicago, Illinois. She was 59 at the time, and worked in the home of a judge.

In 1893, the Davis Milling executives boldly decided to risk their entire future with an all out promotion at the gigantic World's Columbian Exposition in Chicago. They constructed the world's largest flour barrel. "Aunt Jemima," in the person of Nancy Green, demonstrated the pancake mix. She kept up lively conversation with the crowds, while making and serving thousands of pancakes.

Nancy Green was attractive, friendly, a good storyteller, and an excellent cook. Her ability to project her warm and appealing personality made her the ideal "Aunt Jemima," the living counterpart of the company's trademark. She was such a sensation that special details of policemen had to be assigned to keep the crowds moving at the Aunt Jemima exhibition booth.

Davis received over 50,000 orders from merchants all over America and foreign countries. Fair officials awarded Nancy Green a medal and certificate for her showmanship, and proclaimed her the "Pancake Queen." Davis signed her to a lifetime contract, and she traveled on promotional tours all over the country. Because of Nancy Green's fame, her arrival was usually announced on giant billboards. The Davis Company prospered and, by 1910, the name of "Aunt Jemima" was known in all 48 states and had attained such popularity that many persons tried to infringe on the trademark rights.

Until the emergence of Aunt Jemima Pancake Mix, the bulk of flour sales were made in the winter. After the success of the Nancy Green promotion, flour sales were up year-long and pancakes were no longer considered exclusively for breakfast. The Davis Company later ran into money problems and had to sell, but Nancy Green maintained her job until she was accidentally killed by a car on Chicago's south side, on September 24, 1923.

Millions of dollars have been raised through pancake sales for charity. The Boys Club at Rockford, Illinois was built and operated solely from funds raised yearly by Rockford Kiwanians and the Aunt Jemima product. In 1925, the Aunt Jemima Mills were purchased by the Quaker Oats Company of Chicago. In the image of "Aunt Jemima," the Nancy Green legend lives on.

MATTHEW ALEXANDER HENSON
1866-1955

On April 6, 1909, a "20 year odyssey" ended when two Americans planted the American flag at the top of the world. Matthew A. Henson was co-discoverer of the geographic North Pole.

Henson, the son of free-born parents, was born in Charles County, Maryland, in 1866. He was orphaned at an early age and was raised by an uncle in Washington, D.C., where he attended grammar school. At the tender age of 13, he took the position of cabin boy on the merchant vessel *Katie Hinds* for six years. He became an able-bodied seaman, read avidly, and traveled the world over: across the Pacific to the China Sea, across the Atlantic and into the Baltic Sea, stopping in China, Japan, North Africa, Spain, France and Russia.

In 1888, Henson met Commander Robert E. Peary, then a civil engineer in the U.S. Navy, and was more than ready to join Peary's historic expedition. Henson was recommended to Peary as a valet, but Peary soon realized that Henson's ability to chart a path and handle a ship made him invaluable as a colleague. During a Congressional inquiry, Peary admitted that the expedition was greatly aided by Henson's expertise, "I couldn't get along without him. His adaptability and fitness for the work, and his loyalty made him a better man than any of my companions. He is a better dog driver and can handle a sledge better than any man living except the 'best' Eskimo hunters."

Peary took Henson on all his expeditions from 1891 through 1909. During this period, Henson became a jack-of-all-trades, including navigation trading with the Eskimos (who had a great respect for Henson), walrus hunting, and building sledges and igloos in sub-zero temperatures.

On April 6, 1909, accompanied by four Eskimos, Peary (White) and Henson (Black) were the first Americans to reach the North Pole. The conditions these men faced were dreadful. For the final 68 days of the expedition, it became so cold that their hoods froze to their growing beards, and they had to stop to break away ice which had "formed from their breaths and moisture from their perspiration. Snow could not be used for drinking, because it would have reduced the body temperature and caused immediate death." In the face of these horrors, Henson drew upon reciting the *Twenty-Third Psalm* and the fifth chapter of *Matthew.* Henson possessed the unique ability to merge into and even master his environment to the extent of "enjoying the good and enduring the bad."

Upon returning from the North Pole, because of his race, Henson was initially denied his well-deserved recognition. He was employed as a clerk in the New York Customs House, from 1913 to 1936, by order of President Taft. In 1937, he was made a member of the Explorers Club, and was awarded a M.S. degree from Howard University in 1939.

In 1944, Congressional medals were awarded to Henson and the five White men, who started but did not complete the 1908 expedition. In 1948, Henson was awarded a gold medal from the Geographical Society in Chicago. Henson was honored in ceremonies at the Pentagon by President Truman in 1950, and at the White House by President Eisenhower in 1954.

Henson died in 1955; he was survived by his wife, Lucy, and a sister. In 1961, six years after his death, the State House of Annapolis, Maryland passed a bill providing for a bronze plaque crediting Henson as co-discoverer of the North Pole.

JAMES WELDON JOHNSON
1871-1938

James W. Johnson was a well-educated man with exceptional talents; he was a teacher, lyricist, consul, author, editor, poet, and powerful civil rights activist.

He was born in 1871, the second of three children, in Jacksonville, Florida. His father was of mixed ancestry from Virginia, and his mother was of French and Black Haitian ancestry, born in Nassau, Bahamas, and educated in New York City. She taught at the city's largest grammar school for Blacks, and it was she who inspired Johnson's early interest in music and reading.

There were no high schools for Blacks in Jacksonville, so his parents sent him to Atlanta for his secondary and college education, in 1887. Johnson was an outstanding student. While at Atlanta University, he wrote about thirty poems and also delivered the graduation oration in 1894. He returned to Jacksonville and became principal of the local grammar school, which through his efforts grew to become a high school. While teaching, he studied law and became the first Black lawyer admitted to the bar in the State of Florida.

Johnson left a lasting impression on the cultural and social life of the Negro in America. His writing credits are extensive. In 1902, his song *"Under The Bamboo Tree"* sold more than 400,000 copies. He wrote his first novel in 1912. He is credited with writing the renowned Black National Anthem, *Lift Every Voice And Sing* in 1900; the light opera, *Toloso;* and translated into English, the Spanish grand opera, *Goyescas.*

Johnson also wrote music for the exclusive Klaw and Erlarger productions: *The Sleeping Beauty and Humpty Dumpty.* Some of his songs were published in the *Ladies Home Journal,* and many of his articles were published in the

Encyclopedia Britannica. His diplomatic career included being consul to Puerto Cabella, Venezuela in 1906; Corinto, Nicaragua in 1909; and the Azores in 1912.

Johnson resigned his post as consul and became involved with the NAACP from 1916 to 1930. In 1920, he went to Haiti to investigate charges of great brutality to the native people under the American occupation. His stay was short, but he was able to produce facts, for the American public, which led to a congressional investigation. Shortly after, Johnson spent two years in Washington, D.C. trying to secure the passage of an anti-lynching bill in the House of Representatives. Through his efforts, startling and gruesome facts were entered in the *Congressional Record.* After several months, the House passed the bill, but it was later defeated in the Senate.

Johnson took this defeat as a near victory because during the investigations, the truth emerged and the American people had been enlightened. He further sought to strengthen the NAACP. His field work in the south led to the organization of the Dixie District, which added 13 new branches and 738 new members. These branches made the NAACP the strongest organization engaged in the battle of equal rights for Blacks.

After retiring from the NAACP, Johnson became a professor of creative literature at Fisk University. He resumed his writing and began college lecturing at Northwestern, the University of Chicago, Yale, North Carolina, Oberlin and Swarthmore. On several occasions, Johnson became overworked and was forced to take leaves of absence. On one such leave, he met with a tragic death. On June 17, 1938, while driving through a blinding rainstorm, his car was struck by a train at an unguarded railroad crossing. He died almost immediately.

During his lifetime, Johnson, a multi-faceted man, was bestowed with many honors, citations and honorary degrees, but his greatest honor and highest monument was the joy he received from laboring for his people.

◼◼ WILLIAM ALEXANDER LEIDESDORFF ◼◼
1810-1848

William A. Leidesdorff was a pioneer in the development of California. He owned a 35,000 acre estate, captain a 160-ton schooner, and he was also an American diplomat. He built San Francisco's first hotel, opened the State's first public school, introduced the first steamboat and official horse race to California. Leidesdorff became the first Black millionaire in America.

Born in 1810, in the Virgin Islands (St. Croix), he was one of three sons born to a Danish father and an African mother. He and his two brothers were sent to New Orleans to work in their father's cotton business. Sometime later, for reasons unknown, his brothers died and Leidesdorff inherited the capital from the business. In 1841, he left New Orleans (legend has it) because of an unsuccessful love affair and sailed to California on the *Julia Ann*, his 160-ton schooner.

In a short time, Leidesdorff made major changes in California. As recalled by William Tecumseh Sherman in 1847, "California had been without a shod horse, tavern, hotel, or even a common wagon road." Leidesdorff obtained land grants from the Mexican government for two 300-foot lots, and built a store and a home, where he entertained the socially accepted and high ranking political figures. Later, wishing to obtain more land, he became a Mexican citizen and acquired a 35,000-acre estate in 1844. It was located on the banks of the American River, near Sutter's Mill, the birth place of the California gold rush. He named the ranch Rancho Rio de Los Americanos.

The last Mexican mayor of San Francisco gave him another parcel of land in 1846, on what has now become Leidesdorff and California Streets. Upon this land, he built a warehouse and leased it to the U.S. government. By this time he had become a member of the city council, chairman of the school board and city treasurer of San Francisco. During the interim, California was in the middle of a three-way power struggle between the Mexican government, who owned it, and the United States and Great Britain, who wanted it. Leidesdorff played an exciting and influential role, a double agent of sorts, in the political struggle.

In spite of his new citizenship, Leidesdorff conferred with John C. Fremont and other American sympathizers on more than one occasion, to discuss the impending seizure of California by the American government. In July, 1846, the United States Marines seized the city and planted the American flag in the plaza. The night before, Leidesdorff translated the take-over proclamation for the benefit of citizens who did not understand English. Further, Mexican officials were expecting the invasion and had given their flag and official papers to him for safe-keeping. Two weeks later, Leidesdorff threw a fancy dress ball for the conquering Americans. He was allowed to maintain his official posts and was further given the position of American consul.

Leidesdorff's career and fame was short-lived. He died on May 18, 1848, at age 38 of brain fever (typhus). But before his death, he had become a man of great political and social influence. His land holdings and financial wealth were astounding. After a lengthy legal battle, his estate was sold to a White army captain, Joseph Folsom, for $75,000; however, it was later valued at $1.5 million.

BIDDY MASON
1818-1891

Biddy Mason rose to prominence after she challenged a California court and won freedom from slavery for herself and family in 1856. Earning $2.50 a day, she supported three daughters, and also managed to save money to buy land, which came to be worth $300,000. She was a philanthropist, and is best remembered for her charitable works throughout Los Angeles.

According to the Mason family Bible, Bridget "Biddy" Mason was born August 15, 1818 in Hancock County, Georgia. In 1851, her master, Robert Smith, decided to head west and try his luck in the California gold fields. Biddy Mason, at age 32, walked from Georgia to California behind a 300-count, ox-drawn wagon train. In the rear, she strode across the prairie choking in a billowing dust cloud, herding several hundred cattle and sheep with a long stick. The overland journey took six months. Added to this incredible task was the responsibility of caring for three young daughters.

Smith and his slaves stayed in San Bernardino until 1854. Fearing he might lose his valuable "property," Smith decided to take his slaves and family to Texas, and en route, stopped for a few days in Los Angeles County. When the local sheriff, Mr. Frank Dewitt, learned that this slave-master was taking his slaves from the free state of California into the slave state of Texas, he issued a writ against Smith preventing them from leaving. With the good sheriffs help, the courts of Los Angeles County granted Biddy Mason and her children their freedom January 19, 1856. Judge Benjamin Hays declared, "All men should be left to their own pursuit of freedom and happiness."

Biddy Mason settled down in Los Angeles and found work as a confinement nurse for Dr. Griffin, earning $2.50 a day. She worked long, hard hours, lived frugally and managed to accumulate a nest egg of $250.00. She bought two parcels of land in what was considered the outskirts of town; however, today they represent two of the most valuable pieces of property in all of Los Angeles' splendor. Biddy Mason had a fine sense for business matters, and she continued to buy land and retained it until Los Angeles began to boom. She sold her first 40-foot lot for $12,000, and later sold another 40-foot lot for $44,000. In a matter of a few years, she amassed a fortune.

Biddy Mason was a humanitarian, helping those less fortunate than she in anyway she could. She donated land for schools, churches and hospitals; she also paid taxes and expenses on these properties for the sake of her people. She made frequent visits to state jails, always leaving a word of cheer and a small gift with each prisoner. When a flood in the 1880s left many people homeless, Biddy Mason opened a line of credit at a local grocery store for the victims, and cheerfully stood behind all purchases.

When she passed, she left a vast number of friends, both Black and White. As noted in her obituary by the *Los Angeles Times,* "Biddy Mason died January, 1891, at the age of 73, after 40 years of good works."

DR. JAMES W. C. PENNINGTON
c. 1809-1870

Dr. James Pennington, a fugitive slave, was a teacher, clergyman, author, and one of the earliest non-violent civil rights activists. Denied the privilege of a formal education until age 21, within five years after his flight from slavery, he taught himself to read and write English, German, Latin and Greek. Later, he authored the first Negro history text in America, and became the first man of African descent to receive a Doctor of Divinity degree.

Most historical accounts of Dr. Pennington's life are based on his autobiography, The *Fugitive Blacksmith,* in which he recorded his cruel experiences of slavery and described his escape to the north. The book was published in London, in 1849, and went through three editions.

Pennington was born in Maryland in 1809. At the age of 4, he and his mother, plus older brother were given to his master's son and taken to Washington County. Pennington was hired out as a stonemason and a blacksmith. In 1830, when he could no longer endure slave brutality, he ran away to Pennsylvania. There, he was aided by Quakers, who sent him to Long Island, New York. Pennington diligently pursued an education, and within five years began teaching in Black schools.

Later, feeling he had received a calling from God, Pennington went to New Haven, Connecticut and entered a theological seminary. He was ordained and became a proficient preacher of the Presbyterian faith. In Hartford, Connecticut (1840-47) where he won distinction, he was made president of the Union Missionary Society, a forerunner of the American Missionary Association, which urged its members not to buy slave-produced goods.

Pennington was elected twice as president of the all-White Hartford Central Association of Congregational Ministers. During his presidency, it was one of his duties to give examinations in the knowledge of church history and theology to those wishing to become ministers and to sign their certificates accordingly. It must have been a novel scene to see a run-away slave granting the sons of his oppressors leave to go forth and preach the Word of God Almighty. He was elected five times to the membership of the General Convention for the Improvement of the Free Colored People.

In 1843, the state of Connecticut elected Pennington as a delegate to attend the world's Anti-Slavery Convention. He was also elected a delegate by the American Peace Convention to represent them in the World's Peace Society, both held in London. In all, he made three trips to London. His pulpit brilliance won notoriety and many complimentary press notices. While abroad, he preached and made speeches in the presence of some of the most refined and aristocratic audiences of Europe, including London, Paris, and Brussels.

Some historians indicate that his third trip abroad was in 1850, when the *Fugitive Slave Act* was passed. Fearing recapture as a ran-away slave, a fact he had not mentioned to his wife, he left the states until a fee of $150.00 was made to his former master and he was officially freed on June 5, 1851. Further, historians say that during this period, he was awarded the Doctor of Divinity degree by the University of Heidelberg, Germany, the first Black man to receive such an honor.

Pennington organized the New York Legal Rights Association and led his church in some of America's earliest peaceful demonstrations. Through the NYLRA, he instituted a lawsuit against the Sixth Avenue Railroad Company for the right of Blacks to use public conveyances. Although the suit was unsuccessful, the association's action did eventually achieve a degree of equality within the city's transportation system.

Before his death in Florida in 1870, Dr. Pennington expended great energies in denouncing every affront to first-class citizenship.

BILL PICKETT
1870-1932

Bill Pickett has been called one of the greatest Black cowboys that ever lived. He attained national and international fame as a rodeo performer, and is credited with originating a rodeo sport, called "bulldogging."

Bill Pickett, born December 5, 1870 in Williamson County, Texas, was the second of thirteen children of Thomas Jefferson and Mary Elizabeth Pickett, former slaves. After completing the fifth grade, Pickett was hired as a ranch hand, where he developed his skills in riding and roping. Years later (1890), he took a wife, Maggie Turner, and fathered nine children.

In the west, shortly after the Civil War, a new kind of hero began to dominate the American scene, cowboys emerged. They were gutty and tough, and among them was Bill Pickett. He was one of the best. There was not a four-legged beast alive he would not take on. He earned special billing and the professional nickname "Dusky Demon" for his daring bulldogging techniques. Bulldogging was a term given to the act of roping and wrestling steers to the ground. Pickett personalized the sport with exact timing, coupled with guts and power. One reporter is quoted as saying, "Pickett was a man who outdoes the fiercest dog in utter brutality."

The sport of wrestling steers or bulls down by hand goes back to the Roman era. However, Bill Pickett, standing five feet seven inches tall and weighing only 145 pounds, with powerful shoulders and arms, was widely known for his special "bulldogging" skill which he used to compensate for his stature. He would actually sink his teeth into the rebellious animal's nose or upper lip to render it docile and throwable. It is said that Pickett acquired his technique from once witnessing a bulldog "hold" a ranch steer.

In 1907, Pickett contracted with Zack Miller, owner of the famous 101 Ranch and Wild West Show, headquartered in Oklahoma. The 101 Ranch encompassed a hundred thousand acres and employed about 200 cowboys. Miller boasted that he had the best collection of riders and wranglers in the west. Such notables as Will Rogers and Tom Mix got their start at the 101. In a short time, Pickett became the star performer and principal attraction. For over a decade, he performed his daring stunts in the United States, Canada, Argentina, England and Mexico. Only he was bold and powerful enough to tackle a steer, or any other beast, without a lariat.

At a Mexican rodeo, in 1908, Pickett experienced a grueling encounter which almost cost him his life. Zack Miller announced to a crowd of 25,000 Mexicans that Pickett would bulldog a fighting bull. To demonstrate his confidence in Pickett's ability, Miller wagered in excess of $5,000. Pickett accepted the challenge and the match was on. He was tossed about like a ragdoll, but Pickett hung on for dear life. The crowd became hostile and began to bombard him with bottles and stones. They took this as an "insult" to their national sport.

Although Pickett and his horse (Spradley) were severely hurt, Miller won his bet. Shortly after 1916, Bill Pickett retired from the rodeo arena and later bought a 160-acre ranch. In 1931, the 101 Ranch was in serious financial difficulties and he returned to lend a helping hand to his old boss.

One morning while roping horses, Pickett was kicked by a stallion, and died 11 days later of a fractured skull on April 2, 1932. He was buried at the White Eagle Monument, in Marland, Oklahoma, and a marker was erected by the Cherokee Strip Cowboy Association.

Zack Miller declared that Bill Pickett was the "greatest sweat-and-dirt cowhand that ever lived-bar none." In 1971, the legendary "Dusky Demon" became the first Black cowboy to be admitted to the National Rodeo Hall of Fame in Oklahoma City.

George Washington, founded the city of Centralia, Washington. Without any formal schooling, he taught himself to read and write; he was frequently recognized for his skill in math. He was also noted as an excellent marksman with rifle or revolver, and acquired skills as a miller, distiller, tanner, cook, weaver and tailor.

George was born August 15, 1817, of mixed parentage, in Frederick County, Virginia. His father was a Black slave and his mother was White. Shortly after George's birth, his father was sold to another master and George's mother gave him to a White family, the Cochrans, to raise until adulthood. In the early 1820s, George and his adopted parents moved to Missouri, then later to Illinois.

In both states, George was faced with insufferable racial discrimination. He owned a sawmill in Missouri, and when a White customer refused to pay him for a load of lumber, George took him to court. The case was thrown out because Blacks had no legal rights to sue a White person. Later, in Illinois, he was forced to leave because he couldn't afford to pay a $6,000 bond for good behavior, which Blacks were required to pay in order to live in the state.

In 1850, George and his parents headed west to Oregon territory. The journey was rugged and took 117 days by wagon train. On a chosen site, he built a home for his parents and took a job as a lumberjack. He staked his claim on a 640-acre spread, at the junction of the Skookumchuck and Chehalis Rivers in 1851. At the time, Oregon belonged to the Indians, but Whites took matters into their own hands and tried to forcibly eject the Indians off the land and to ban all Blacks. George knew of the White's intentions to take his land, and he stood to lose all he had worked for. He had his White parents (the Cochrans) file a claim in their name, and George later sold them his improvements on the land for $200.

In 1853, the Oregon territory became the Washington territory, and George was able to buy back his property for $3,200. At that time, the Indians were at war. All the White settlers, including his parents, fled to Fort Henness for protection. George remained on his land without fearing harm. He was friends with the Indians and they respected him. They called him *"Noclas"* meaning "black face," or *"Myeach"* meaning "charred wood." In 1869, George married Mary Jane Cooness.

In 1872, the Northern Pacific Railroad ran across Washington's land, and he then decided to establish a town. He named it Centerville, since it was half way between Kalama and Tacoma, but later changed the name to Centralia. George filed a four-block square plat with intentions to recruit other settlers. He sold lots for $5 and $10, with the stipulation that owners had to build a house worth at least $100 on their property. George's wealth and property grew tremendously.

In 1889, Mrs. Washington died; George married Charity Brown in 1890, and fathered a son. He built a church, a school, rental houses and other needed buildings. He also designated land for a cemetery and public park. These improvements attracted a steady flow of newcomers.

From 1893 to 1897, Centralia suffered an economic depression, and hundreds of settlers began to leave. To save the city, George established himself as a one-man relief agency. He provided the settlers with rice, flour, sugar, meat, clothing and other items. He even furnished money to those who needed it to pay mortgages, loans and other debts. To his credit, Centralia survived and became prosperous again.

Washington died on August 26, 1905, and a day of mourning was proclaimed. The Centralia, Washington public park, which was donated by George Washington, today bears his name.

WILLIAM WHIPPER
1805-1885

William Whipper, a leading Black intellectual, was a famed abolitionist, shrewd businessman, and banker. He was also one of the earliest advocates of the non-violent movement in America, 12 years before Thoreau wrote his famous essay on civil disobedience, and a hundred years before Gandhi and Dr. Martin Luther King, Jr. made the theory world-famous.

William Whipper was born in 1805, the son of a Columbia, Pennsylvania White businessman. His mother was a Black domestic slave in his father's household. He was raised in his father's house and was treated much the same as his White half-brother. Early in life, he was given the opportunity to acquire sound principles of financial investment and management. His father left him a small lumberyard when he died. With his partner, Stephen Smith, Whipper built a successful wholesale business which expanded to other cities in Pennsylvania.

Whipper became an active participant in the anti-slavery movement. In 1835, he was the prime mover of The Moral Reform Society, designed to unite "free people of color." This was done either by helping people of color adopt agricultural pursuits in the United States, or by helping them move to the Province of Canada. For more than a decade, Whipper used his own money, and collected funds from his White friends to assist the Society in its efforts.

In the 1850s, during a time when most Blacks could not own property, the company of Whipper and Smith had accumulated 27 of the most sought-after "merchantman" cars on the railroad. Further, at a time when private citizens could build bridges and charge for public use, Whipper and his associate made a $9,000 investment in the building of the Columbia Bridge. They also bought $18,000 worth of stock in the Columbia Bank of Pennsylvania.

At that time, their lumberyards housed over 2,250,000 feet of lumber and their warehouses held thousands of bushels of grain. Smith became one of the wealthiest Blacks in America because he devoted his energies only to the business aspect of their partnership; conversely, Whipper chose to share his wealth with the Black movement.

In 1870, Whipper stated, "I would prefer to be penniless in the streets, rather than have withheld a single hour's labor or a dollar from the sacred cause of liberty, justice, and humanity." He gave considerable sums of money to help Black slaves and to aid the Union during the Civil War. In the 1880s, Whipper devoted much of his personal time and money to the Negro Convention Movement, the first nationwide effort by Blacks to plead their cause in America.

Whipper, the forerunner of Thoreau, Ghandi and Dr. King, advocated moral suasion and non-violence. He wrote a famous article, entitled *An Address On Non-Resistance To Offensive Aggression,* which was published in the *Colored American.* In it, he claimed that non-violence is not only consistent with reason, but the surest method of obtaining a speedy triumph of the principles of universal peace.

William Whipper died in 1885, but his doctrine of non-violence is still practiced by many present-day contemporaries.

NOTES

TEST YOURSELF

Now that you have familiarized yourself with our historic Black Pioneers, in this third series of Empak's Black History publications, this section, in three parts: MATCH; TRUE/FALSE; MULTIPLE CHOICE/FILL-IN, is designed to help you remember some key points about each notable Black Pioneer. (Answers on page 28)

MATCH

I. *Match the column on the right with the column on the left by placing the appropriate alphabetical letter next to the pioneer it represents.*

1. Bill Pickett _____
2. Carter G. Woodson _____
3. James P. Beckwourth _____
4. Clara Brown _____
5. Barney Ford _____
6. James W. Johnson _____
7. Abraham _____

A) Founded a church in Colorado
B) Hotel Tycoon
C) Indian counselor
D) Black national anthem
E) Historiographer
F) Bulldogging sport
G) Mountain pass
H) Gunslinger

TRUE/FALSE

II. *The True and False statements below are taken from the biographical information given on each of the pioneers.*

1. Mary Fields was the first female ever to drive a U.S. mail coach. _____
2. Paul Cuffee started the first public school in San Francisco, California._____
3. George Washington was a one-time chief of the Crow nation._____
4. James Johnson became the first Black lawyer admitted to the bar in the state of Florida._____
5. Jean Baptiste Pointe DuSable is recognized as the "Father" of Chicago, IL._____
6. Esteban, the first Black man to lead a spanish expedition, is credited with discovering the states of Arizona and New Mexico._____
7. The Noted historian, Carter G. Woodson, fought for the colonization of free Blacks to Sierra Leone, Africa._____

MULTIPLE CHOICE/FILL-IN

III. *Complete the statements below by drawing a line under the correct name, or by filling-in the correct answer which you have read in the biographical sketches.*

1. (Clara Brown, Barney Ford, Biddy Mason) challenged a California court and won the family's freedom in 1856.
2. James Pennington was the first person of African descent to receive a _____ _____ degree.
3. Matthew Henson was the co-discoverer of the _____ on April 6, 1909.
4. "Aunt Jemima," in the person of _____ was the advertising world's first living trademark.
5. (Abraham, Crispus Attucks, James Johnson) was the first to die in the Boston Massacre on March 5, 1770, which is synonymous with the independent birth of America.
6. In 1875, (George Washington, William Whipper, George Bush) founded an American town called _____
7. _____ was the forerunner of the non-violent movement long before the arrival of Gandhi and Dr. Martin Luther King, Jr.

CROSSWORD PUZZLE

ACROSS

1. *Under The Bamboo Tree*
5. Moral Reform Society
7. Underground Railroad
9. Breakfast treat
10. *"Traveller"*
11. 49th Parallel
13. Taxation without Representation
14. 600 mile trek
15. Northern exposure
16. Double agent
17. A man of the "cloth"
18. "Seven Cities of Cibola"

DOWN

2. "Legends never die"
3. Real estate fortune
4. "Dusty Demon"
6. "Keeper of the King's conscience"
8. Great Lakes trader
11. "Bulls Robe"
12. One-man relief agency
13. Harvard Ph.D.

WORDSEARCH

1. Abraham
2. Crispus Attucks
3. James Beckwourth
4. Clara Brown
5. George Bush
6. Paul Cuffee
7. Jean Baptiste DuSable

8. Esteban
9. Mary Fields
10. Barney Ford
11. Nancy Green
12. Matthew Henson
13. James Johnson
14. William Leidesdorff

15. Biddy Mason
16. James Pennington
17. Bill Pickett
18. George Washington
19. William Whipper
20. Carter Woodson

The names of our twenty HISTORIC BLACK PIONEERS are contained in the diagram below. Look in the diagram of letters for the names given in the list. Find the names by reading FORWARD, BACKWARDS, UP, DOWN, and DIAGONALLY in a straight line of letters. Each time you find a name in the diagram, circle it in the diagram and cross it off on the list of names. Words often overlap, and letters may be used more than once.

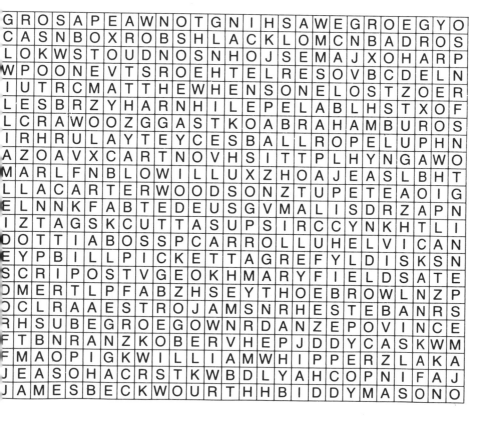

MATCH

1.–F	5.–B
2.–E	6.–D
3.–G	7.–C
4.–A	

TRUE/FALSE

1.–FALSE	5.–TRUE
2.–FALSE	6.–TRUE
3.–FALSE	7.–FALSE
4.–TRUE	

MULTIPLE CHOICE

1.–BIDDY MASON	5.–CRISPUS ATTUCKS
2.–DOCTOR OF DIVINITY	6.–CENTRALIA
3.–NORTH POLE	7.–WILLIAM WHIPPER
4.–NANCY GREEN	

CROSSWORD PUZZLE

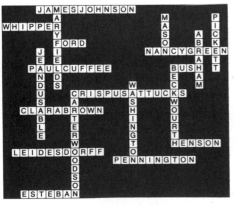

WORD SEARCH

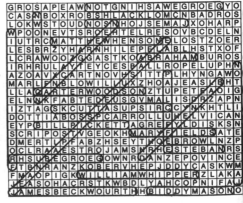

Name _____

Affiliation _____

Address _____
P. O. Box numbers not accepted, street address must appear.

City _____ State _____ Zip _____

Phone# (_____)_____ Date _____

Method Of Payment Enclosed:　( ) Check　　( ) Money Order　　( ) Purchase Order

Prices effective 11/1/95 thru 10/31/96

ADVANCED LEVEL

Quantity	ISBN #	Title Description	Unit Price	Total Price
	0-922162-1-8	"A Salute to Historic Black Women"		
	0-922162-2-6	"A Salute to Black Scientists & Inventors"		
	0-922162-3-4	"A Salute to Black Pioneers"		
	0-922162-4-2	"A Salute to Black Civil Rights Leaders"		
	0-922162-5-0	"A Salute to Historic Black Abolitionists"		
	0-922162-6-9	"A Salute to Historic African Kings & Queens"		
	0-922162-7-7	"A Salute to Historic Black Firsts"		
	0-922162-8-5	"A Salute to Historic Blacks in the Arts"		
	0-922162-9-3	"A Salute to Blacks in the Federal Government"		
	0-922162-14-X	"A Salute to Historic Black Educators"		

INTERMEDIATE LEVEL

Quantity	ISBN #	Title Description	Unit Price	Total Price
	0-922162-75-1	"Historic Black Women"		
	0-922162-76-X	"Black Scientists & Inventors"		
	0-922162-77-8	"Historic Black Pioneers"		
	0-922162-78-6	"Black Civil Rights Leaders"		
	0-922162-80-8	"Historic Black Abolitionists"		
	0-922162-81-6	"Historic African Kings & Queens"		
	0-922162-82-4	"Historic Black Firsts"		
	0-922162-83-2	"Historic Blacks in the Arts"		
	0-922162-84-0	"Blacks in the Federal Government"		
	0-922162-85-9	"Historic Black Educators"		

Total Books			
		❸ Subtotal	
		❹ IL Residents add 8.75% Sales Tax	
SEE ABOVE CHART ▷		❺ Shipping & Handling	
GRADE LEVEL: 4th, 5th, 6th		❻ Total	

BOOK PRICING ● QUANTITY DISCOUNTS

Advanced Level	Intermediate Level
Reg. $3.49	Reg. $2.29
Order 50 or More	Order 50 or More
Save 40¢ EACH	Save 20¢ EACH
@ $3.09	@ $2.09

❺ SHIPPING AND HANDLING

Order Total	Add
Under $5.00	$1.50
$5.01-$15.00	$3.00
$15.01-$35.00	$4.50
$35.01-$75.00	$7.00
$75.01-$200.00	10%
Over $201.00	6%

In addition to the above charges, U.S. territories, HI & AK, add $2.00. Canada & Mexico, add $5.00. Other outside U.S., add $20.00.

Name _____

Affiliation _____

Street _____
P. O. Box numbers not accepted, street address must appear.

City _____ State _____ Zip _____

Phone (_____)_____ Date _____

Method Of Payment Enclosed: ( ) Check   ( ) Money Order   ( ) Purchase Order

Prices effective 11/1/95 thru 10/31/96

PRIMARY LEVEL... KINDERGARTEN, FIRST, SECOND & THIRD GRADE				
Quantity	ISBN #	Title Description	Unit Price	Total Price
	0-922162-90-5	"Kumi and Chanti"		
	0-922162-91-3	"George Washington Carver"		
	0-922162-92-1	"Harriet Tubman"		
	0-922162-93-X	"Jean Baptist DuSable"		
	0-922162-94-8	"Matthew Henson"		
	0-922162-95-6	"Bessie Coleman"		
	Total Books		❸ Subtotal	
			❹ IL Residents add 8.75% Sales Tax	
		SEE CHART BELOW ▷	❺ Shipping & Handling	
			❻ Total	

KEY STEPS IN ORDERING

❶ Establish quantity needs.
❷ Determine book unit price.
❸ Determine total cost.
❹ Add tax, if applicable.
❺ Add shipping &handling.
❻ Total amount.

BOOK PRICING ● QUANTITY DISCOUNTS

❶ Quantity Ordered	❷ Unit Price
1-49	$3.49
50 +	$3.09

❺ SHIPPING AND HANDLING

Order Total	Add
Under $5	$1.50
$5.01-$15.00	$3.00
$15.01- $35.00	$4.50
$35.01-$75.00	$7.00
$75.01-$200.00	10%
Over $201.00	6%

In addition to the above charges, U.S. territories, HI & AK, add $2.00. Canada and Mexico, add $5.00. Other outside U.S., add $20.00.

Empak Publishing provides attractive counter and floor displays for retailers and organizations interested in the Heritage book series for resale. Please check here ☐ and include this form with your letterhead and we will send you specific information and our special volume discounts.

- The Empak "Heritage Kids" series provides a basic understanding and appreciation of Black history which translates to cultural awareness, self-esteem, and ethnic pride within young African-American children.

- Assisted by dynamic and impressive 4-color illustrations, readers will be able to relate to the two adorable African kids -- Kumi & Chanti, as they are introduced to the inspirational lives and deeds of significant, historic African-Americans.

Black History Materials
Available from Empak Publishing

A Salute To Black History Poster Series
African-American Experience–Period Poster Series
Biographical Poster Series
Heritage Kids Poster Series

Advanced Booklet Series
Instructor's Manuals
Advanced Skills Sheets
Black History Bulletin Board Aids
Instructor's Kits

Intermediate Booklet Series
Teacher's Guides
Intermediate Skill Sheets
Black History Flashcards
Intermediate Reading Certificates
Teacher's Kits

Heritage Kids Booklet Series
Heritage Kids Resource & Activity Guides
Heritage Kids Reading Certificates
Heritage Kids Kits

Black History Videos
Black History Month Activity & Resource Guide
African-American Times–A Chronological Record
African-American Discovery Board Game
African-American Clip Art
Black History Mugs
Black Heritage Marble Engraving
Black History Month Banners (18" x 60")
Say YES to Black History Education Sweatshirts
Say YES to Black History Education T-Shirts

To receive your copy of the Empak Publishing Company's
colorful new catalog, please send $2 to cover postage and handling to:

Empak Publishing Company
Catalog Dept., Suite 300
212 East Ohio Street
Chicago, IL 60611